50 Hound-Dog Man 50 The Evolution of a State 50 The House of Breath 50

Texas History Movies 50 The Butterfield Overland Mail 50 Pale Horse, Pale Rider 50 The Bone Pickers

Goodbye to a River 50 Interwoven 50 Sam Bass 50 Horseman, ...

The Fifty Best Books
on Texas

A. C. GREENE

Dallas   Pressworks Publishing   1982

...d Autumn in Your Hand

50 Coronado's Children 50 A Ranchman's Recollections 50 The Gay Place 50

Contents

These are, my choice, the 50 best Texas books—and I'd like to emphasize, they are my choice because I like them. I would also like to emphasize that these are the best books *about* Texas. By that I mean, Texas is their main subject or, in the case of fiction and biography, their chief setting. They are not the best books written by Texas authors (in fact, not all the authors are Texans) and they may not be the most important Texas books—but don't let's get off into a thicket of objectives and explanations: the quality of the books speaks for itself. They are the best.

When this idea was first proposed, it was suggested that a list of the best 100 Texas books be made. But I said no. While 100 good titles could be assembled, 100 opens the door too widely. So, 50 it is.

I have not used any particularly stringent criterion for including a book save for the rather inexact one of "good." And, incidentally, the books are not listed in sequence of preference or ranked in any other way. I have not attempted to pick something from each form of literature, but I haven't slighted any type of writing, either, unless you might say I excluded textbooks and technical manuals. But, frankly, if I had been attracted to a book of that sort, I would not have hesitated to include it.

I am not guilty of picking books written by friends. True, I know and like (or knew and liked) several of the authors whose works I have chosen, but as you will discover if you read the notes on the individual titles, I have not been universally liked by those whose books I have chosen. Knowing the author shouldn't make a book better, or worse, in one's critical judgment.

I

There are a number of fine Texas writers not represented on my list of 50 best books. In virtually every case it is because they have not written books about Texas. That certainly explains the absence of a title by Frances Mossiker or Leon Harris (although Leon came close with his famous adaptation, "The Night Before Christmas; In Texas, That Is"). Donald Barthelme, a notable Texan of letters, has done only a few short stories involving his Texas antecedents. Marshall Terry, a Texan most of his life, wrote a small masterpiece, *Tom Northway*, but old Tom lived his 90 years in Ohio.

There are certain books one might think would appear automatically on a list of Texas best, for example, *The Devil Rides Outside* by the late Texas writer John Howard Griffin; but again, it's not about Texas. Bill Goetzmann's *Exploration and Empire* won the Pulitzer history prize, among others, and established a new way of writing western history, but, alas, has less than a tiny portion on Texas. Edward Weems' *To Conquer a Peace* is the most readable thing done on the Mexican War, but once more, Texas is a minor part of its history.

The 50 best of Texas will change through the years—my own choices will change if I live a few more years, I am sure. Some titles may make other lists in later days: Elmer Kelton's *The Time It Never Rained* and Stephen Harrigan's *Aransas* I feel pretty sure of; Andrew Jolly's *A Time of Soldiers*, and Gary Cartwright's *Blood Will Tell*, could easily score, and so might Harry Hurt III's *Texas Rich: The Hunt Dynasty*.

There was one book I planned to include until I read the author's introduction (to the Time Reading Program edition). That was *The Sea of Grass*, by Conrad Richter. Even Frank Dobie thought it was a Texas book when he first read it (according to Richter), but the author specifically denies the Texas taint.

Someone may ask, what about Edna Ferber's *Giant*? I happen to think *Giant* is a bad book; a spiteful piece, crippled by the author's regional ignorance and her inability to separate Hollywood caricature from Texas character. Any other questions? Well, there's *The Wind* by Dorothy Scarborough. *The Wind* is a ridiculous novel telling how those bad ol' West Texas elements drove mad a gentle Virginia blueblood cast out on the frontier. Perhaps she had a right to go mad, being powerless to leave the narrative and escape the author's non-stop, three-year (honest to God!) sand storm. Come to think of it, both heroines—of *Giant* and of *The Wind*—were Virginia FFVs. Maybe Virginia ladies should stay out of Texas fiction?

There are other books I wish I could stick in regardless of scant Texas references, just because so few people know they have any Texas references at all; books like Thornton Wilder's *Heaven's My Destination* and Arthur Lewis's *The Day They Shook the Plum Tree*, delightful reading. Then, there are books such as *The Death of a President* by William Manchester, the best known of the Kennedy assassination books, or the Warren Commission report itself; wherever they might belong, I have left them out.

I have not included any sets, although one could argue that Thomas W. Streeter's *Bibliography of Texas 1794–1845* in five volumes is as good as any historical work done on Texas. But one has to draw a line. I have not included any of the Cabeza de Vaca narratives, or reports from the early Spanish expeditions. For that matter, I've shied away from almost all history-as-history books. Many are quite valuable, but this s not the 50 most *valuable* books about Texas.

There are some titles missing which are standard entries in "Texas Best." Most are cowboy and cattle industry books, such as *We Pointed Them North, Riata and Spur, Log of a Cowboy, Trail Drivers of Texas,* or *The Cowboy and His Interpreters.* They are excellent research sources (I've used them all), but, again a personal observation, I think Texas has moved out of the part of its historic past which includes so many range and cattle books. They once represented a considerable segment of interest of a considerable segment of Texas population. Not any more. The same thing is true of frontier folklore; it's fading, as are most of the books it produced. In fact, I've never been much on folklore—it has a perverse way of jumping from one region to another by merely changing local names. Fun to read, but hard to lay much store by.

In the matter of editions—with most books I have listed the first edition; more as a matter of historical interest than anything else. In a few I have gone to other editions because first editions are untouchable or subsequent editions are better. Later editions are available in a good many of these titles. I have not chosen any book because of its rarity. Several of the books I have picked as "50 Best" are available in softcover, and if that suits your taste, feel free; I am not a hardcover snob, although I prefer them. On the other hand, I have not let scarcity stop me from listing a title. A few may be hard to locate, even in Texas libraries—I might say, particularly in Texas libraries; Texas libraries, like Texas universities, are fearful of a "regional" tag stuck on them.

Some may ask, why Texas books? Is Texas afraid to stack its art against the general literary art of the nation? Well, Texas is certainly big enough to have its own art; it's larger than a good many important nations. And Texas is one of the few states of the United States that retains a separate identity—for reasons historical, cultural, and political. Part southern, part southwestern, it is neither when it comes to writing about itself. Jump over the border to Louisiana or New Mexico—or even to Oklahoma—and you run into a completely different kind of writing and storytelling . . . different in style, in implications, in what it is striving for.

But I wouldn't for one moment stand up and declare Texas writing greater than the differences. Unfortunately, Texas has not furnished indigenous materials for great novels like LaFarge's *Laughing Boy*, Frank Waters's *The Man Who Killed the Deer*, or Bandelier's *Delight Makers*, as did New Mexico. It has drawn out no *Death Comes for the Archbishop*, and few products comparable to Richard Bradford's *Red Sky at Morning*.

Texas writing, generally, lacks subtlety. Texas is not a subtle place; its societies have not been subtle. Direct, open, candid—the stuff of legend, but not necessarily of literature. Texas writers have been better at telling what was done than what was thought—or what was felt. To know what a Texan did has, most often, been to know what he thought. Texas has always enjoyed asking lots of questions of itself, but it has always gone to the mirror for its answers. Texas takes great delight in studying its reflection in the mirror—even the funhouse mirror. A Texan feels he always has something to fall back on, if the questions get uncomfortable: being a Texan.

How long will this list of "50 Best" hold up? I can't guess. There are two significant developments which will change literary values in Texas, including mine. First, Texas has attracted a whole tribe of new writers, some already established in American letters, some returning home, and some compelled to try and create artistic emotions to match their cultural excitement—Texas song writers and playwrights have already succeeded along this latter line. And the black writers of Texas will have more and more to say about their Texas, past and present—this applies also, of course, to the Hispanic or the Indian writers, making books, stories, poems, plays

5

which may surpass in quality a number of works I include here. Texas is changing rapidly its ways and its tastes. The urbanization of Texas is the next great chapter in Lone Star literature.

And finally, I hope I have not sounded too arbitrary with bold assertions: "... this is my pick ... my choice is ... this is the best." But I feel there hasn't been enough of this in Texas letters. I think Texas has needed some positive criticism, more outspokenness from within, as regards its own culture. The bold international braggart, when it comes to material trivia, Texas has an inferiority complex about its art. Behind that mask of bigness, Texas can't believe there is the ability to bring forth, in and of itself, something worthy of mankind's recognition. Texas has relied too long and too completely on the opinions of others.

Do I have the qualifications to make this kind of listing and these comments? Well, as for the first point, I've read everything I endorse, and most of what I have left unnoted. And for what it's worth, I have lived in Texas most of my born'd days and have been intimately associated with Texas writing, books, and authors—not to mention critics, editors, and publishers—for several decades.

But, lacking anything else, I boldly submit my choice for Texas' 50 best books. And, outraged or in agreement, give you leave to make your own.

DALLAS, 1981

The Fifty Best Books on Texas

Coronado's Children

by J. FRANK DOBIE

Southwest Press, Dallas, 1930

This is the book that made it possible for a Texas writer to stay home and make a living. When *Coronado's Children* was published (in Texas), it was picked up by the Literary Guild—first non-Eastern publication ever chosen by the Guild or Book-of-the-Month—and became a national success. The book created Frank Dobie's "Mr. Texas" image which stayed with him for the rest of his life. Although the Guild payment was a pittance by today's standards (and his Texas publisher went bankrupt before paying him full royalties), the consequences of all this were more valuable than dollars. First off, Dobie got a Guggenheim grant which enabled him to take off and do *Tongues of the Monte*, but more important, he could now sell anything about Texas he wanted to write; and this opened the field for others, too.

Coronado's Children is folklore about lost mines and buried treasure, caves full of gold bars, and jack-loads of Spanish silver. (How many of us had heard of a jack-load before we read Dobie?) I know of no other Texas book from which so many feature writers have filched so much.

When I met Frank Dobie some twenty-five years after first reading *Coronado's Children*, I told him it was still my favorite of his books. He acted hurt. I think friends convinced him his more serious works, like *The Longhorns* or *The Mustangs*, better fit his literary stature. Or maybe it was Mrs. Dobie. After his death, when I was a Dobie-Paisano Fellow living on his ranch, we became friends, and I suspect Bertha wished he were more of a footnote-counter. Bless her gracious memory, I'm glad he wasn't.

Southwest

by

JOHN HOUGHTON ALLEN

Illustrated by Paul Laune

J. B. LIPPINCOTT COMPANY
PHILADELPHIA AND NEW YORK

Southwest
by JOHN HOUGHTON ALLEN
Lippincott, Philadelphia, 1952

This collection of autobiographical essays about an older lifestyle on the border of South Texas defies description. Frank Dobie, in his *Life and Literature of the Southwest*, can scarcely restrain himself from going after Allen. John Houghton Allen writes with great sympathy for the people and the lands where he lived, but he writes more like a nobleman than a rancher. The short stories (or pieces) in *Southwest* are subtly tinged with that air of privilege, of being birth-appointed to a role in history that may be tragic, but was necessary. That's not the tone one expects to find in Texas ranch tales. His gentlemen ranchers (and their spoiled sons) are as devoted to horses as to wives—with the exception, now and then, of other men's wives. The Mexican ranch hands and their folklore go back to Spanish times, and privilege comes naturally—an inheritance passed along by the Spanish ranchers who settled the kingdom of the Rio Grande in the eighteenth century to the dynastic Anglos who superseded them—or stole their titles and their privileges. But *Southwest* is a fascinating, unusual book about Texas that isn't duplicated by any other writer. Reading it is like reading about a foreign country; Randado is akin to Brigadoon, and fantasy fits snugly within Allen's romantic style.

Hound-dog Man

BY
FRED GIPSON

Harper & Brothers Publishers
NEW YORK

Hound-Dog Man
by FRED GIPSON
Harper & Brothers, New York, 1949

Fred Gipson came very near to writing a Texas *Huckleberry Finn* in *Hound-Dog Man*. It was his first book-length fiction, and as is generally the case with first-books, he crowds several stories in it, particularly the Boy-grows-up and Natural Man-gets-tamed stories, which involve the youngster Cotton and Blackie Scantling, the hound-dog man. Gipson makes both stories work: Cotton is more than just a frontier boy undergoing the huntsman's rites of passage, and Blackie becomes more (or, in his case, less) than the woodsman corraled by the love of a good woman.

Gipson's sensitive passages about nature are far above much Texas writing on such matters, but his passages about people are even more evocative, and it is his handling of Blackie that shows his artistry, because otherwise *Hound-Dog Man* would be, like *Old Yeller*, just a good juvenile. I have always suspected that Blackie was a kind of reverse-image of Gipson, particularly Blackie's way with (and view of) women. Gipson denied it, laughingly, one long week end a clutch of us spent gossiping at Paisano, not too long before he died. I didn't change my mind.

Some readers class this a children's book. Nonsense. The title isn't *Cotton Learns Life* . . . the title is *Hound-Dog Man*.

*Original Narratives of
Texas History and
Adventure*

ఆు

THE EVOLUTION OF
A STATE

By NOAH SMITHWICK

ఆు

A FACSIMILE REPRODUCTION OF THE ORIGINAL

ఆు

THE STECK COMPANY
AUSTIN, TEXAS
1935

The Evolution of a State
Or, Recollections of Old Texas Days
by Noah Smithwick
Gammel Book Company, Austin, 1900

There just is not a better or more human document of early days in Texas than Noah Smithwick's. He dictated it to his daughter when he was in his nineties, and blind, and had not lived in Texas for nearly forty years. But the great humaneness of the man overcame those drawbacks—that and his good memory. Smithwick was not well educated, but he was (as the saying goes) keenly observant. He came to Texas in 1831, got banished for a while, then was back to see the Republic survive and become a State. Smithwick rose above the general pettiness of so many Texas colonists. He forgives easily, and on more than one occasion he sides with the Indians and with Negroes who had been unjustly or prejudicially handled. He seems particularly fair about Negroes, in a day that was seldom understanding. Smithwick shows a keen sense of humor, not the least about himself. But he is no respecter of persons; he refers to the sainted Col. William Barrett Travis of Alamo memory, as Bill, and opines "he had not the qualities necessary to a commander." There is scarcely a name in Republic of Texas history he doesn't mention personally. With the inevitability of the Civil War, Smithwick, a Democrat but a Unionist, sold everything and fled to California. He never returned to Texas, dying in California in 1899 at age 92. His book is not about heroes, it is about everyday people. He recites only what he knows. "Theories and conjectures are not evidence," he writes. If I could recommend only one book of early Texas, it would be *The Evolution of a State*.

A TEXAS RANGER

AND

FRONTIERSMAN

The Days of Buck Barry
in Texas

1845-1906

Edited by
JAMES K. GREER

THE SOUTHWEST PRESS
DALLAS, TEXAS
1932

A Texas Ranger and Frontiersman
The Days of Buck Barry in Texas 1845-1906
Edited by JAMES K. GREER
The Southwest Press, Dallas, 1932

Texas pioneers were not all God-fearing, hardworking, and honest. If you think they were (because Grandpa was), then James Buckner Barry's memoirs will not only change your mind—it might make you want to change your name. Buck Barry arrived in Texas in 1845, age 24, on the second steamboat ever to dock at Jefferson. He became a Texas Ranger, was the first sheriff of Navarro County, and then participated in a series of Indian fights, vigilante episodes, and (as he saw it) other forms of community service. He didn't like horse thieves (he hung several), dishonest lawyers, and cowardly judges and jurors, all of whom he encountered. But Buck was fair, and there's not a word of self-praise in his journal. One of his greatest values to history came during the Civil War when he was head of Confederate frontier battalions, ranging across the length and breadth of West Texas, telling about it in detail. Buck's home base (a farm he traded a gold watch for) was Walnut Springs on the Bosque River. It's a part of the state little explored by historians. Modern readers may not find Buck Barry's attitudes and views entirely lovable, especially concerning Indians. But while he didn't sympathize with them, he treated them as honorable foes, never sneering at them or projecting them as mere savages to be exterminated.

James K. Greer assured me, twenty years later, that his editing of Barry's journals included a great deal more than just deciphering his handwriting, that old Buck had some things to say that just couldn't be loosed on the world.

BLESSED McGILL

Edwin Shrake

Doubleday & Company, Inc., Garden City, New York
1968

Blessed McGill

by EDWIN SHRAKE

Doubleday, Garden City, N.Y., 1968

Edwin (Bud) Shrake, like so many authors, started out as a news-paper sports writer. In fact, when I went to work for the Dallas *Times Herald* and met him in 1960, he, Blackie Sherrod, and Gary (Jap) Cartwright were on the same staff, joined, or succeeded im-mediately, by Dan Jenkins and Steve Perkins . . . you talk about a Golden Age of sportswriting. But all the time, Bud was writing novels, a good many of which seemed to be reaching for some truth about life (Texas life) that needed to be explained. *Blessed McGill* combines the best of Shrake's talents: an appreciation for the ab-surdities of existence, a recognition of irony's major role in the world, highly suggestive humor, and a decent amount of historical and anthropological research so that the book never spews off into campy pseudo-historical "nonfiction" that characterizes a whole school of American prose. *Blessed McGill* is hilariously funny. It begins with a boy in Austin, Peter Hermano McGill, growing up following the Civil War, reared by a devout (but a little cuckoo) Catholic mother. Through circumstances, he becomes as much a brother to the Indians as to Anglo society—guarded by a renegade half-breed and a Karankaway throwback called Badthing. But Shrake does not sacrifice truth or wisdom for sheer entertainment, and when McGill—by a series of inevitabilities—moves toward sainthood in Taos, it is not merely an absurd plot twist, but a subtle study of what spiritual deliverance really is.

A Ranchman's Recollections

by FRANK S. HASTINGS

Breeders' Gazette, Chicago, 1921

The thing you have to watch out for, wading through a lot of Texas ranch and cattle books, is (how can I put it politely?) the hogwash. Famous ranchers (and their biographers) sometimes took themselves quite seriously, implying an importance to, if not outranking, Stephen F. Austin and Sam Houston; neglecting the idea that their heroic stature was usually based on free land and legal chicanery. But Frank Hastings tells about the cattle industry, not ranching. The industry didn't begin with the romantic longhorns, it began with the meat packers who created the real market for the ranchers' cattle—which quickly became Herefords. Hastings was not a cowboy. University trained, he worked for Armour Packing, became internationally famous for his knowledge of bloodlines, and in 1902 was made manager of the SMS Ranches of Texas, where he helped change ranching from a gambler's adventure to a business science. But his book is even more readable and exciting than run of the range memoirs because it is informed, and charming with accuracy.

I once won a case of Old Crow whiskey by submitting a poem (about Old Crow) I found in *A Ranchman's Recollections* to the distillery's advertising agency. I lived in a dry territory, but I was sent a letter instructing any liquor dealer to honor the bequest. I hesitantly showed the letter in a Fort Worth store, to be greeted by: "We've been looking for you." The Fort Worth dealers had been notified of the letter, and this store, located on the highway from my dry home, sensed it would be the one I hit. I advised the manager to read *A Ranchman's Recollections* when he expressed curiosity about the event.

Interwoven

by SALLIE REYNOLDS MATTHEWS

Carl Hertzog, El Paso, 1958

A number of charming women wrote books, or portions of books, about their experiences in Texas: Mary Austin Holley, Jane Cazneau, Amelia Barr, Libby Custer, Melinda Rankin, to name some. But Sallie Reynolds Matthews, in *Interwoven*, gives us a lifetime view, not that of a visiting journalist or traveler. And what she gave tells more about daily life on the frontier than any comparable narrative. Sallie was not only bright, she caught and understood the eternal rhythms of society which do not change. Born in West Texas in 1861, she tells of girls and boys in love, foolish but lovable brothers and (a few times) husbands, of weddings and babies—but never in a sentimental vein. This is a delightful book, written around the Reynolds and Matthews families which intermarried and whose affairs were (and are) so bound together as to be inseparable, justifying the title. It is also the history (and good history) of a large part of the cattle frontier from the 1860s to modern times. Without setting out to do so, she shows us the differences between that Texas society and ours—which lifts *Interwoven* out of the family memoir class to become a historical tool.

I have chosen the Hertzog edition—the first was in 1936—because it is, to me, the most beautiful specimen of his work: design, type, choice of artists, even a specially designed fabric for binding with "M/R" interwoven. My copy is a unique binder's trial, given me by the late H. V. Chapman, of Abilene, who bound several Hertzog classics. It has two errors on the endpaper map: Ft. Bel(k)-nap and Shackle(el)ford County. They do not appear, of course, on the final printing. I have resisted some stout offers.

Sam Bass

By WAYNE GARD

WITH ILLUSTRATIONS

BOSTON AND NEW YORK

HOUGHTON MIFFLIN COMPANY

The Riverside Press Cambridge

1936

Sam Bass

by WAYNE GARD

Houghton Mifflin, Boston and New York, 1936

Sam Bass is still the most popular bandit in Texas history, probably because of the song about him. Fact can never overtake legend, not in the case of an outlaw someone has written a song about, but fact is, Sam wasn't a very successful bandit. He made only one big haul, and that was in Nebraska. But in Denton County, his Texas home, there are still plenty of people who hold Sam Bass to have been a frontier Robin Hood, and in 1972, when I was working on a local history, I was proudly shown half a dozen spots which family history (read tradition) said were where Sam hid out, buried treasure, or performed some deed of kindness, usually to a pore widderwoman. What Texans liked about Sam Bass was the fact he wasn't mean. He was a good-natured, careless, likable young fellow, who died of Texas Ranger gunshot wounds on his twenty-seventh birthday in 1878. His grave is near Old Round Rock. I visited it one winter day when no one else was in the cemetery. A man in a car watched me the whole time. He told me he was protecting the tombstone. Through the years souvenir hunters carried off several stones, in pieces.

Wayne Gard's life of Sam Bass doesn't fall into the folklore trap, although it relates the more prevalent tales along with the facts. Wayne never forgets he is writing about a man whose facts are unimportant in comparison to what he didn't do. It is readable and reliable—the most reliable account of Sam Bass.

by Larry McMurtry

HORSEMAN, PASS BY

Harper & Brothers *Publishers* New York

Horseman, Pass By

by LARRY MCMURTRY

Harper & Brothers, New York, 1961

I was a book review editor when *Horseman, Pass By* came out and I might not have read it had it not been for my younger brother, David, who picked up my review copy from a tall stack and said, "I knew this guy in North Texas." Oh, looking back, I guess I would have read it because I certainly would have looked through a new Texas book, and if so would surely have caught the rhythm and truth in the writing, because it is about a world I knew from carrying it under my fingernails, and any page would have struck a chime of recognition in me.

Horseman, Pass By views a changing scene and the people in it; contrasting heroic frontier virtue with down-to-earth effectiveness; mythology with reality. The book speaks through the mind and eyes of Lonnie, a boy watching his heroic West Texas ranch world sway and explode, while his ideas of manhood go through the same process. The movie made from the book, *Hud*, shifts emphasis from Lonnie to his arrogant, almost cruel—but ultimately the savior—uncle, Hud Bannon. It works well in the movie, but the book retains the art. This was McMurtry's first book and while it won the Texas Institute of Letters fiction award (which dismayed some members) it wasn't a major success. I'm rather proud to have spotted it before most reviewers. In fact, McMurtry wrote me a letter (before we met) saying he thought my review was the best one the book got.

TEXAS
HISTORY MOVIES

Illustrations by JACK PATTON
Text by JOHN ROSENFIELD, JR.

TURNER COMPANY
DALLAS  TEXAS

Texas History Movies

Illustrations by JACK PATTON, Text by JOHN ROSENFIELD, JR.

P. L. Turner Co., Dallas, 1928

Along with a couple of generations of Texans, I got my start in loving state history from *Texas History Movies* in comic strip form. The most popular edition was a small paperback that came out in the 1930s, distributed by Magnolia Petroleum Co. by the thousands throughout the Texas school systems. Jack Patton, the illustrator, was a well-known cartoonist with the *Dallas Morning News* and John Rosenfield became the foremost Texas music and drama critic in his long service with the same paper. In their foreword, Patton and Rosenfield say that while remaining historically correct, they "directed every effort to keeping the stories humorous, human, vivid and real [but have not] scrupled to use slang, colloquialisms, and deliberate anachronisms to project what [we] believe to be the spirit of an episode." In later years *Texas History Movies* was criticized for depicting Mexican leaders in harsh caricature, and Mobil Oil (which absorbed Magnolia) dropped distribution, giving the printing plates to the Texas State Historical Association. The history holds up very well, incidentally.

A few years before his death, and nearly forty years after *Texas History Movies* first appeared, I asked John Rosenfield if he'd made a fortune off it, and he said no, quite the contrary. The book had orignated as a series in the Dallas *News* and, when put in book form, nobody expected the success it enjoyed. Besides, the publisher went broke.

27

AL DEWLEN

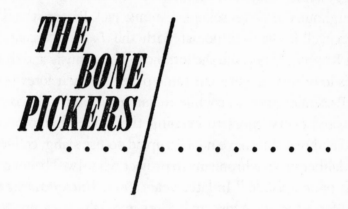

THE BONE PICKERS

McGRAW-HILL BOOK COMPANY, INC.

NEW YORK
TORONTO
LONDON

The Bone Pickers

by AL DEWLEN

McGraw-Hill, New York, 1958

When the buffalo were hunted off their Panhandle range in about four years time, the old big-bore Sharps killers moved on, leaving piles, mountains, of bones for the pioneer settlers to pick up, haul to the railroad, and make a living off of. For a while, in both West Texas and the Panhandle, it was the only way the settlers could survive, but there was nothing noble about it, and most families didn't brag about doing it the way the old buffalo killers bragged, later on, about slaughtering the herd in statistical ecstasy. Well, *The Bone Pickers* isn't a historical novel about the Panhandle (unless the time of the 1950s is already history—which, I hate to admit, it is), but it fits the historical metaphor, because it is the long dissolution of the Munger family of Amarillo, wealthy beyond count from the ravagings of old crazy Cecil, but shattered down to bone pickers in his descendents, most of them (Spain, China, Laska, Texas) named for geography—old Cecil loved to read the atlas aloud to his family, after he'd played them a few danceable hymns on his harmonica— try waltzing to "Whispering Hope." But don't let this brief interlude make you think this is another Faulknerian family dynasty novel. The Mungers are both modern and sane—oh, except for June, who has to have an ex-cop keeper. And the story of the family's descent is a corporate one, mixed with political connivance and a touch of civil rights abuse. Jealousy, vanity, and the pressures of money all figure in the lengthy saga—which doesn't cover many years but lots of pages. Al Dewlen's novel still has certain residents destroying copies, I've been told.

The
BUTTERFIELD
OVERLAND MAIL

By
WATERMAN L. ORMSBY
*Only Through Passenger on
the First Westbound Stage*

Edited By
LYLE H. WRIGHT AND JOSEPHINE M. BYNUM

THE HUNTINGTON LIBRARY
San Marino, California
1942

The Butterfield Overland Mail

by WATERMAN L. ORMSBY
Edited by Lyle H. Wright and Josephine M. Bynum
The Huntington Library, San Marino, California, 1942, 1955

Waterman Ormsby was the first, and only, through passenger on the first westbound Butterfield Overland Mail Company stage in 1858. He was a young reporter for the New York *Herald*, and he sent back first-person feature stories of his progress along that first transcontinental mail line, which stretched from Tipton, Missouri, through Arkansas, the Indian Nations, Texas, New Mexico, and Arizona, to San Francisco. Ormsby was a good reporter and a good writer. He noticed things. He was witty and tolerant, disposed to be amused rather than infuriated at some of the exciting, or ridiculous, events, places, and people he encountered on the maiden voyage of the historic Butterfield stage—which was national news because it set a record for crossing North America. Since much of the Butterfield route was across Texas, the state occupies a great chunk of Ormsby's delightful narrative.

In 1958 I followed the Butterfield Trail through North and West Texas as a centennial project celebrating that first run, and, Ormsby's dispatches in hand, I discovered them to be not only accurate, but almost as usable as they had been a century earlier, places along the remote trail had changed so little.

KATHERINE ANNE PORTER

PALE HORSE,
PALE RIDER

Three Short Novels

hb

HARCOURT, BRACE AND COMPANY, NEW YORK

Pale Horse, Pale Rider

by KATHERINE ANNE PORTER

Harcourt, Brace, New York, 1939

Some may say *Pale Horse, Pale Rider* is not a Texas book, but they forget, perhaps, that the volume of that title contains two other famous short novels, *Old Mortality* and *Noon Wine*, both with Texas settings. But, in any case, I don't care. I insist *Pale Horse, Pale Rider* is the best Texas fiction ever written. The story takes place during World War I, but it is as contemporary as any feminist work since. Miranda, a newspaper reporter (who, as a young girl, is also in *Old Mortality*) hasn't a taint of outdatedness; she is headstrong and independent, yet gentle and, despite herself, romantic. But none of this gentleness allows her to be pushed around—except by a terror bigger than Miranda is.

Katherine Anne Porter, the one time I met her, denied acidly she had been a newspaper reporter in Dallas—or Texas. I have always thought it strange she was so bitter in her disavowal of things Texan, yet did so many of her best stories with a Texas background. (I once spent half a day trying to find her birthplace in Brown County.) Katherine Anne Porter told an interviewer, shortly after *Pale Horse, Pale Rider* was published, she could not really imagine "creating" a story; that everything she had written or would write must be based firmly on a foundation of actual experience. Who knows?

Triggernometry

by EUGENE CUNNINGHAM

Caxton Printers, Caldwell, Idaho, 1934

I made my first acquaintance with gunmen and badmen in *Triggernometry*, which despite that trivial sounding title is a reliable, excellent book. Badmen attracted my imagination from an early age
because my great-grandmother (who more than half raised me) was
Bill Longley's stepmother. I don't want to sound too romantic
about it; she never knew the gunman, having married old Cam,
his daddy, after Bill was hanged—or was he? Texas tradition, and
Longley family legend, claimed he left the country and a hog was
substituted for his body in a coffin . . . but that doesn't have much
to do with the quality of *Triggernometry*. I only know I accepted
everything in it as fact, and some twenty years after first reading it
was delighted (and relieved) to find that Frank Dobie vouched for
Cunningham's knowledge and the book's authenticity.

Charles Goodnight: Cowman and Plainsman

by J. EVETTS HALEY

Houghton Mifflin, Boston and New York, 1936

This remains the best Texas biography I've read, although on the whole, I've never cared much for writing that glorifies the pioneers, despite having been raised, in part, by an archetypal frontier granny. Charles Goodnight scrambled from orphan poverty to ultimately being the greatest cattleman of them all. He had imagination, respect for ability, and sensitivity toward nature and other men—but through it all he was basically a hardheaded businessman. He was a myth, but he wasn't a mythmaker. Goodnight came to Texas in 1846 at age ten and died in 1929, so his life spanned the legendary history of the cowboy and rancher. He fought Indians innumerable times, he scouted for the Texas Rangers, he trailed longhorns to Colorado and Kansas—but he also opened a college so his ranch families could be educated, he helped save the American buffalo from extinction, and he helped (reluctantly, perhaps) bring civilization to the Texas Panhandle. There was no one like him.

J. Evetts Haley wrote the Goodnight story from first hand. It is as flamboyant, and as down to earth, as its subject; but it isn't worshipful. Its glory is its readability—with scholarly footnotes. He wrote many other books, but none touches *Charles Goodnight*. Mr. Haley was once outraged at a review I did of one of his books (the abominable *A Texan Looks At Lyndon*). At a press conference he called me "a journalistic prostitute." I could never bring myself to get very upset about it.

Adventures with a Texas Naturalist

ROY BEDICHEK

Illustrations by WARD LOCKWOOD
Foreword by H. MEWHINNEY

UNIVERSITY OF TEXAS PRESS AUSTIN

Adventures with a Texas Naturalist
by ROY BEDICHEK
Doubleday & Co., Garden City, N.Y., 1947

Roy Bedichek, although older than they were, was considered a sort of creation of Frank Dobie and Walter Prescott Webb, when all three were sharing company in Austin. Dobie and Webb forced Bedichek to isolate himself and write *Adventures With a Texas Naturalist,* spending a winter in an upper room at Webb's Friday Mountain Ranch. The book that resulted was worth their trouble, for Bedichek writes like an ancient Roman on some pages, like a charming philosopher on all pages, and combines enough of the Texas storyteller to suit the reader who doesn't care a hoot about the *havardi* oak or Baruch Spinoza's observations on God and nature.

Bedichek never lets a topic confine him. He wanders off into unbelievable fields of thought no matter which Texas natural wonder he observes or describes. He stops and chats with the reader, not in a traditional Texas "voice" but almost as a classics instructor, yet almost never failing to insert some tale or anecdote. Without Thoreau's political asides, Bedichek offers nature as the best solution to mankind's private despairs. Old fashioned, but not outdated, the book forces one to acknowledge Texas cannot really be known without reading *Adventures With a Texas Naturalist*. Ironically, it could easily outlive most of the books of Bedichek's mentors.

Journal of the Secession Convention of Texas 1861

Edited from the original by ERNEST W. WINKLER, State Librarian

Texas Library and Historical Commission, Austin, 1912

This is the most tragic document in Texas history, and the most dramatic. Officially, and meticulously (469 pages, not one of them wasted), it details the enveloping tornado which swept even Texans with better sense into the catastrophic history known as "The Southern Cause." Although these official minutes are, without the slightest question, pushing pell-mell to disaster, we see the galleries full (literally) of cheering supporters as folly succeeds folly: the counting of votes, the naming of delegates, the resolutions, speeches, motions, braggadocio, letters, reports, brave and foolish acts, grandiose Confederate schemes. Why couldn't sanity have been allowed, just one day, or in one session, to rise above the malarkey, the empty rhetoric? Because, at this point, in Texas, to have opposed Secession would have meant total dishonor (as happened to Sam Houston) or even death. The *Journal of the Secession Convention* makes all this plain, without commentary. Its compressed chronology pushes it along like a brilliant historical novel. The Secession Convention (illegal in its inception) was called for January 1861, and by March 25 when it adjourned, Texas was committed to the cataclysm that destroyed, perhaps forever, the chances of these United States to be a happy union.

The Great Plains

by WALTER PRESCOTT WEBB

Ginn & Co., Boston, 1931

Although *The Great Frontier* is supposed to be his broadest contribution to history, and *The Texas Rangers* is more purely about Texas, my preference among Walter Prescott Webb's books is *The Great Plains*. Its scope reaches far beyond Texas—beyond the United States, for that matter—but it is Texas inspired, and it explains more about Texan culture, even today, than just about anything written, or shown on television. Webb's idea of a unique plains civilization and its effect on history is a true contribution to social history without bogging a reader down in social science jargon (which is particularly deadly when mixed with history—as happens so often today). Sometimes *The Great Plains* even sings, something none of Webb's other books do unless an individual reader recognizes a challenging idea is being presented to him for the first time. I think Webb wasn't taking himself so seriously as an international scholar when he wrote *The Great Plains*—a posture more evident in *The Great Frontier*, which can get downright unreadable. I must admit, some of my difficulties with Webb's writings may have a personal genesis. I found him almost unapproachable the few times I tried to converse with him. Those who know him better said this was the impression of many persons, but assured me it was wrong.

13
DAYS TO GLORY

THE SIEGE OF THE ALAMO

by Lon Tinkle

McGRAW-HILL BOOK COMPANY, INC.
New York   Toronto   London

13 Days to Glory
by LON TINKLE
McGraw-Hill, New York, 1958

Lon Tinkle was the most courtly man of letters Texas has produced, but he had strange little fears. When Walter Lord's intensive study of the battle of the Alamo, *A Time to Stand*, came out in 1961, I stated in a review that whereas Lord's work is more inclusive and historically evaluative than Lon's *13 Days to Glory*, I preferred the Tinkle book because it is more revealing. While factually sound, it explores the mystery of what kept those men at the Alamo to die, as Lord points out, somewhat needlessly. I got a phone call that afternoon from Lon Tinkle expressing his gratitude, but also his wonder, that I made the statement. Since we were, at that time, book critics on competing Dallas newspapers, he had quivered (his word) all week that I might seize the opportunity to elevate the fine Lord book and denounce that of my rival. (Those who recall his matchless diction can hear his voice on that sentence.) I was the one to quiver a few weeks later when I introduced Walter Lord at a book and author luncheon; but he made only an amused reference to the review, as we parted: "Oh . . . that."

13 Days to Glory gives the essence of the Alamo story without attempting to exhaust history's explanation. Tinkle is fair to the Mexican attackers, even Santa Anna, and does not hallow the slain Texans; neither does he insist all the legends are true. But the strange consensus of the defenders to stay and die, he implies— and that is what makes the book such uncommonly good reading.

This Stubborn Soil

WILLIAM A. OWENS

Charles Scribner's Sons   New York

This Stubborn Soil

by WILLIAM A. OWENS

Charles Scribner's Sons, New York, 1966

Texans tend to think pioneer biography was written (or lived) only in the nineteenth century. Bill Owens refutes that. His autobiography is about pioneer life in the twentieth century—in an isolated North Texas community with the folksy (but genuine) name of Pin Hook. It was a frontier existence, all right. The automobile wouldn't bring in modern times for another decade. But Owens doesn't indulge in heroic cliche and claptrap about those backwoods pioneers. He enjoyed boyhood (and writes about things like hymn singing and rhyming games) but he realized early on he had to escape—and Pin Hook becomes a metaphor for all the Americans who pulled themselves away from their place of birth in order to transcend its values and dogmas. Owens escaped to Dallas in 1923, at age 18, forced to take any job he could get—and he got precious few breaks —but continually driven by a formless compulsion to go to college, though he left Pin Hook with less than an eighth grade education. But *This Stubborn Soil* is not a Texas success story; it is a story of determination to survive—to survive in a world that is suddenly, and fearsomely, changing. The fact that it is witty, rollicking, and full of appealing innocence places it in a secure literary niche. (And Owens became a longtime professor at Columbia University.)

The Wonderful Country
by TOM LEA
Little, Brown, Boston, 1952

This is a personal observation, but I wish Tom Lea had abandoned painting for writing. He's a good painter, possibly as good a painter as writer, but that's not my point; point is, his writing is a unique product, so superbly attached to a place—or times and cultures in a place—that to have lost even one or two books, as we surely did, to his painting is to have lost forever something that cannot be regiven. In *The Wonderful Country* Tom Lea writes about that lost literary land that corners on Texas, New Mexico, and the Mexican states of Sonora and Chihuahua. El Paso, his birthplace, is situated in the center of it. I happen to prefer this novel to anything he's written because it explains mysteries of motivation that history never delivers. Lea's description of events: dawn, clouds, shadows, sandstorms, cold, dryness . . . hits the reader in each of the reader's senses. Maybe that's the color artist instructing the word artist. Whatever it is, *The Wonderful Country* is a Texas novel almost without flaws, done with an economy of words and emotions. Set in a time slightly before ours, it nonetheless has no antiqueness about it, and the book's main character, Martin Brady (Martín Bredi) is surely one personification of Lea's own ideals.

A Journey Through Texas
by FREDERICK LAW OLMSTED
Dix, Edwards & Co., New York, 1857

Most of the earlyday travel books about Texas read like bad theater or real estate sales brochures. Olmsted, commissioned by the New York *Times* to write about the southern slave economy, came to Texas in the 1850s with a distaste for the institution, but it seldom taints the descriptions of what he finds. He had a trained eye for land and its use (he went back to New York and became chief architect for Central Park) and he had traveled in Europe and China, so he had a tolerance for strange peoples and strange habits—although he never approves of the degradation some Texans allowed themselves to live in. He visited Houston, San Antonio, Austin, Eagle Pass, the German settlements (his favorite settlers) and the coastal towns and plantations. It is perceptive and intelligent reporting and remains good reading. In 1980 I was commissioned to write a brief history of Austin, and I found Olmsted's comment on that city contained an apt title for my own work. He wrote, "Austin [is the] pleasantest place we have seen in Texas." If nothing else, it proves his observations hold up well with time, because that seems to be the way visitors still see things.

Six-Guns and Saddle Leather

A Bibliography of Books and Pamphlets on Western Outlaws and Gunmen

by RAMON ADAMS

University of Oklahoma Press, Norman, 1954

Ramon Adams seemed born to be a compiler, starting in the 1930s with *Cowboy Lingo*, then *Western Words*, going to *Six-Guns*, *The Rampaging Herd* (a bibliography of the cattle industry), *Burs Under the Saddle* and *More Burs Under the Saddle*—the latter pair pointing out the errors, inconsistencies, and deliberate lies to be found in hundreds of western titles. I think *Six-Guns* is the best because it more nearly approaches literature through its subject. After all, detailing the lives and crimes of Southwestern outlaws is a literary contribution in itself; *Six-Guns* can be read for sheer enjoyment of itself, as can both the *Burs* books. After you read *Six-Guns* (which will take you a while, for it is huge) you can feel rather secure in your understanding of the frontier gunman. Ramon Adams was a dedicated man whose life will reward scholars for at least another hundred years, but he could be unforgiving. In reviewing *Burs Under the Saddle*, which, as noted, is about errors in other books, I pointed out a couple or so mistakes in Ramon's book. It took nearly ten years for him to speak to me again, even though I had the honor to hand him a prize check when *Burs* won a major Texas Institute of Letters award. I'm happy to say, he lived long enough to forgive me. Incidentally, Ramon Adams, so identified with cowboys and outlaws, came to Texas originally to play violin in a Dallas theater orchestra. When he injured his hand and stopped playing, he made his living as a candymaker, even after some of his most important books came out.

The Mexican Side of the Texas Revolution
by CARLOS E. CASTANEDA
P. L. Turner, Dallas, 1928

Castañeda was a Mexican by birth but he got his schooling, and spent his professional career (as teacher, librarian and historian), entirely in Texas. His greatest historical work was the seven-volume *Our Catholic Heritage in Texas*, but valuable as this set is, I think Castañeda's best contribution to Texas history was *The Mexican Side of the Texas Revolution*. As the title implies, this is a documentary presentation of what the various Mexican military leaders, and soldiers, had to say about such Texian sore points as the battle of the Alamo, the Goliad massacre, and their defeat at San Jacinto. Not that Mexican eyewitnesses were any more reliable than those across the gunsights from them—in fact, phraseology obscures (purposefully) some of the Mexican reports. But the book is a necessary antidote to the hell-for-leather one-sided version of history Texans ordinarily get. Castañeda (whose loyalties were as much with Texas as with his native land) just presents "the other side," and does it with scholarship and not persuasion. From time to time some recent historian comes up with a new "revelation" about some diary, journal, or report unearthed concerning the Alamo or another item from the Texas revolution; in 90% of the cases, Castañeda (who is not to be confused with the latterday mystic of similar name) had mentioned it.

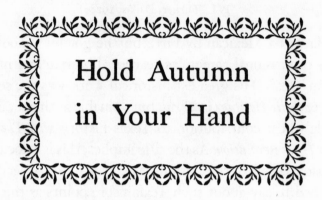

Hold Autumn in Your Hand

BY GEORGE SESSIONS PERRY

The Viking Press · New York

1941

Hold Autumn in Your Hand

by GEORGE SESSIONS PERRY

Viking Books, New York, 1941

Perry was a good writer, and his best writings owe their power to the Texas society and its individuals they describe. *Walls Rise Up* is an amusing novel about two down and out Texans trying to survive in the Brazos bottoms with as little work as possible. But I like *Hold Autumn in Your Hand* because it attempts more. *Walls Rise Up* (published in 1939) is a trifle on the Texas trite side. *Hold Autumn in Your Hand* goes deeper into the character and integrity of Sam Tucker, a Texas tenant farmer in those same bottoms, who, though "too poor to flag a gutwagon," continues to fight nature, the seasons, the river, and a good many of his fellow men, for the satisfaction of bringing something (himself, if you want some philosophy) from the earth, despite never being able to pull back and watch. But it is something more than just another man's fight against nature; *Hold Autumn in Your Hand* is full of country humor—pretty racy, of course—and Texas common sense (presuming it's different from other kinds of common sense). We may have lost that old tie with the earth our immediate forefathers had, but modern readers will find it no barrier to enjoyment. Perry's later disabilities (crippling arthritis) and his unexplained death (his body was found in a Connecticut river two months after he apparently wandered away from his home) ended what was, at the time, the most successful Texan writing career to be found. (*Hold Autumn in Your Hand* was made into a film titled *The Southerner*, with Texan Zachary Scott playing Sam Tucker.)

49

Love is a Wild Assault

by ELITHE HAMILTON KIRKLAND

Doubleday, Garden City, N.Y., 1959

Romantic novels about early Texas history have tended to go more toward the history than toward the development of the characters —although one would think, reading about some of those early day wild men, that the characters would swamp any historical narrative that tried to confine them. But Elithe Hamilton Kirkland handles this provocative situation very well in her books, best of all in *Love Is a Wild Assault*, the love story of Robert Potter and Harriet Moore Page Potter. Potter was a leading political figure in early Republic of Texas times, a stormy outcast from North Carolina. He was something of a poet, but he had a streak of savage fury in him which, mixed with his Moderator-Regulator War involvement and his near-illicit liaison with Harriet, brought disaster. Much of the novel takes place on the gloomy shores of Caddo Lake, with its cypress trees forming dim corridors over the mysterious waters. Potter Point, his home (and still a landmark), is where the climax of that War and his love occurred. The writing is based on the autobiography of beautiful and brave Harriet and on court records of her attempt to show her "bond" marriage with Potter was legal. The book is passionately written because the story was passionately played. This true love story, even fictionalized, makes a fit contrast to some of the Gothic creations of love-in-danger.

The House of Breath
by WILLIAM GOYEN
Random House, New York, 1949

East Texas has had a hard time establishing a proper place for itself in fiction, with Louisiana and the Cajun culture lying just across the lower Sabine and cowboys and Indians belonging altogether to Texas farther west. But William Goyen, in *House of Breath*, created a region of memory which belongs purely to the piney woods, the swamps and mists of that area. Goyen called his town Charity, and he peopled it with characters like Boy Ganchion, whose confessional betrays—at least reveals—the secrets of a dozen or so other characters in town. Charity itself is pictured in almost mythical terms, once a prosperous village with farming and lumber prosperity— and the box factory, which still looms importantly in the town's life, although closed. The elements may sound like misplaced Yoknapatawpha, but Goyen makes them distinctly Texas—East Texas of his creation. Boy Ganchion was also tortured by the necessary repression of his sexual urges, and *House of Breath* created much of a flutter among some Texas literary figures, for it deals with the idea in frank terms, although not with the four-letter overkill we are so inured to since. Regardless of how many Charitys there may be— or may never have been—in East Texas, Goyen created his own landscape, and many a Texas writer tried to become a resident, without success.

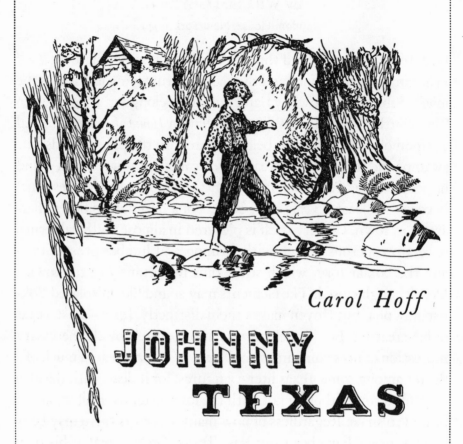

Carol Hoff

JOHNNY
TEXAS

BOB MEYERS ILLUSTRATIONS

Follett Publishing Company CHICAGO

Johnny Texas

by CAROL HOFF

Wilcox and Follett, Chicago, 1950

Had I not been in the book selling business back in the early 1950s, I probably would not have discovered *Johnny Texas*. It is a juvenile, for one thing, and I was a bit beyond that designation. Also, at that stage of my life, I had only one offspring—just born—so there was no one to read books to, or for my wife to read to. That, believe me, is a marvelous way to discover some wonderful books, particularly when you might have jumped over some juvenile classics (as I did) in your haste to grow up. But I sold so many copies of *Johnny Texas* I decided I'd better read it. A lot of Texas juvenile fiction melts into the same youngster visiting a ranch for the first time, the same girl owning the same prizewinning lamb (or calf) destined, alas, for the slaughter pen, or the same youngster wanting to follow in the family ranching boots but Daddy (oilman, lawyer, doctor) doesn't like ranching so Old Bill, the ancient, brokendown former cowboy becomes buddies with young . . . well, *Johnny Texas* isn't like any of those. Johnny is a young German offspring on the frontier who does a man's job with a freight wagon to make enough money for his family to survive. Even Frank Dobie, who only listed a couple of juveniles in his, *Guide to Life and Literature of the Southwest*, called it "delightful."

Blood and Money

THOMAS THOMPSON

Doubleday & Company, Inc.
GARDEN CITY, NEW YORK

Blood and Money

by THOMAS THOMPSON

Doubleday, Inc., Garden City, New York, 1976

There are people who shudder in horror that a book about Houston society murders and associated skullduggery might be taken for literature. But, subject aside, *Blood and Money* is an excellent book, well documented (at least, it has stood the test of legal challenges) and not one the reader puts down, even when the concluding chapters are well known. Its importance does not rest on the series of crimes it may or may not depict; its status is based on Tommy Thompson's very skillful handling of a very unbalanced, ticklish kind of story—one which was not ended (officially) when the book came out and, years later, apparently would have no end. But again, the reader of *Blood and Money* isn't bothered by this fact. *Blood and Money* is a complete work, with reliable asides, and sufficient in itself, no matter what might have come to light—or may yet come to light—concerning the principals.

I had a shock of recognition, reading this book. I discovered I knew an ancillary figure in the tapestry very well at one point in my life, and had met one of the major, tragic characters at another point. Texas is still a small world.

A Texas Trilogy

Preston Jones

The Last Meeting of the
Knights of the White Magnolia

Lu Ann Hampton Laverty Oberlander

The Oldest Living Graduate

A Mermaid Dramabook
 HILL AND WANG • NEW YORK
A division of Farrar, Straus and Giroux

A Texas Trilogy

by PRESTON JONES

Hill and Wang, New York, 1976

Preston Jones had a priceless asset for a playwright—more valuable for a playwright than a novelist. He could absorb an individual or a whole society, squeeze them out one by one or in groups, then return to his original shape, untainted by what had passed through his hands. A good playwright seems to recognize that he is writing for others, both directly, as in the case of the actors, and indirectly, as in the case of the theater audience. A novelist, alas, too often has to write for some inner self that either exhausts or inflates the creator all out of shape. Thus, Preston Jones, after years of urban living and (one accepts) a rejection of his mythical setting of Bradleyville, Texas, can write without rage, yet with deep comic understanding in his three plays: *The Last Meeting of the Knights of the White Magnolia, Lu Ann Hampton Laverty Oberlander,* and *The Oldest Living Graduate.* He lets readers and audiences find happy compromises, sad realities, or ultimate triumphs. A novelist, given the same set of characters and backgrounds, would have had to smash something—a few lives, if nothing else. Yet in reading these plays, or seeing them performed, you know more about the social confusions of our world—the broad world, not a particularly isolated Texas world—and the possibilities for happiness in them, than depths and depths of pop psychology or philosophy can deliver.

Preston's unexpected death in 1979 cut off what should have been a flow of fine drama. I was with him a few nights before, and he was outlining whole areas of theatrical exploration—inspired more by his growing realization of his own power than by the drinks we were having.

ARMADILLO
IN
THE
GRASS

SHELBY
HEARON

ALFRED A. KNOPF

NEW YORK 1968

Armadillo in the Grass

by SHELBY HEARON

Alfred A. Knopf, New York, 1968

To this point, modern, suburban Texas has not had a better social expositor than Shelby Hearon. And while she has written a continuing number of good books, *Armadillo in the Grass* sticks with me as her best. Maybe it has a personal angle; I was living in Austin at the time *Armadillo* came out, and since we shared publishers, I was given advance notice that a hitherto unknown writer was about to make a conspicuous contribution to Texas letters. It took me a bit to find her, but that predicted emergence took care of all that. Before long her name was one of those automatics arising when a list of best Texas writers is called for. *Armadillo in the Grass* catches a moment (of varying minutes, hours, or days) in the life of every woman when she has to ask herself how brave she may be—to change or to stay as she is. Clara Blue, long married, with children, finds unexpected artistry in herself and it becomes a challenge and a fright, because it clearly opens up doors that require others to be closed. The book is subtle, gentle, but strong. No cattle queens, no oil-baron wives, no honky-tonk romances—a real Texas, nonetheless, and a story that is shaped by its Texas setting. And whether the author included parts of herself in Clara Blue or not, *Armadillo in the Grass* made her meet some of the same decisions that faced the artist in the book.

... AND OTHER
DIRTY STORIES

by Larry L. King

Foreword by Willie Morris

An  *Book*

The World Publishing Company
NEW YORK   CLEVELAND

. . . *And Other Dirty Stories*

by LARRY L. KING

World Publishing, Cleveland and New York, 1967

The name of this book was supposed to have been *LBJ and Other Dirty Stories*, but the publishers backed down on that one, LBJ still being President at the time. Be that as it may, I think this collection of profiles and pieces is the best writing Larry King has done. There is a great amount of original power in such ruthless studies as "My Hero, LBJ" and there is a surviving innocence in his remembering his West Texas childhood—particularly "Requiem for a West Texas Town," which writes an obituary not for one tiny (pop. 190) town, Putnam, where he was born, but for that resolute, doomed society in all our Putnams which is being wiped out by such blind forces of civilization as the Interstate Highways. King has written well, and with a vast amount of style, in several other works, but this first collection stands strongest—particularly its Texas portions, which comprise over half its contents.

Although Larry and I were born within forty miles of each other (which isn't any distance in West Texas) and probably saw one another in our youth (given I'm five years his senior), we didn't actually meet until 1966 when I wrote a not-too-kind review of his first novel, *The One-Eyed Man*. King sent a note of appreciation, saying my review was fair and might prove valuable. He suggested we meet soon—we did, and I've had some marvelous experiences (essentially literary in nature) in his company since.

William Brammer

The
Gay Place

being three related novels
The Flea Circus
Room Enough to Caper
Country Pleasures

Houghton Mifflin Company · Boston

The Riverside Press · Cambridge

The Gay Place

by WILLIAM BRAMMER

Houghton Mifflin, Boston, 1961

What can I say, what remains to be said, about *The Gay Place*? It has been overpraised, it has been assigned values it never possessed, and much of the outpouring of acclaim has come from critics motivated by sympathy for the author. But the book is good, in many ways the best modern novel (three novellas, actually) about Texas. The setting is Austin, the vocation of the stories is politics, and the dominant figures are powerful, ruthless politicos—the most celebrated being Governor Fenstemaker, by now universally accepted as a caricature of Lyndon B. Johnson. But when the book was published, Brammer denied Fenstemaker was Johnson. The first time I met him, and his then-wife Nadine, at a snug little publisher's introductory in the old Baker Hotel in downtown Dallas, Billy-Lee (as friends loved to call him) whispered another name, from Texas politics, to me as "the governor." Well, that passed quickly when LBJ became President. Fenstemaker *had* to be LBJ, then. And so he became. *The Gay Place* is a sad book, a fine book, and one that lovingly relates the pawing and snorting of the power structure. In that respect, it holds up beautifully, because Austin, as a political society, never changes. Brammer's skill at sex scenes, the general decay of personalities, and the sadness of the floating life should have made him at least a contemporary Fitzgerald. Billy-Lee had it all. But he couldn't conquer himself (who can, really?) and he never wrote another book. I think too many people loved him, and it killed him twice.

A TIME
AND
A PLACE

Stories by

William Humphrey

A Time and A Place

by WILLIAM HUMPHREY

Alfred A. Knopf, New York, 1968

William Humphrey has been a sort of mystery man of Texas letters. He writes mainly about Texas—his corner being that northeastern portion around Clarksville—but he stays aloof from the scene to such an extent that it takes prize checks from award-giving groups weeks and weeks to find him. But his writing is what counts, not his absence or presence in Texas. *A Time and a Place* is a book of short stories centered on his Clarksville corner. They start before Humphrey himself started (which is early in the 1920s), yet offer full flavor and tonic of their time. Humphrey subtly imparts amusing, intriguing, or (at times) enormously shocking ideas which appear, or are understood, all of a sudden. It is easy to designate stories as "classics," but several of the stories in this book qualify as Texas classics; I particularly like the one about a man who comes to town and climbs the courthouse tower. Humphrey has spent most of his writing life abroad or on the Eastern seaboard (my favorite of his books, *The Spawning Run*, is set in England). I wish he could have spared Texas a few years of residence somewhere in there. His commentary (fictional) on our much changed society could have been priceless.

Uncovered
Wagon

HART STILWELL

1947

DOUBLEDAY & CO., INC., GARDEN CITY, N.Y.

The Uncovered Wagon
by HART STILWELL
Doubleday, Garden City, N.Y., 1947

You think all the old-time Texans worshipped their fathers and learned lessons of manliness and integrity from them? Not necessarily. *The Uncovered Wagon* seems to be written around a core of autobiography, and Billy, the boy in the book, grows up hating and fearing his father, who is called only "the Old Man." Stilwell, who got pretty cranky as he aged, argued loudly and damningly with me when I suggested this, but you don't need an Eskimo to tell you there's ice in Alaska. (Stilwell was an unpredictable cuss, and once at a party where a friend and I were singing and playing hymns, on a guitar and a harmonica, he proceeded to strip off his clothes in protest and sit, stark naked, in the middle of the floor until we stopped. Then he talked.) *The Uncovered Wagon* takes place in those uneasy years just before World War I, and Billy and the Old Man spend a lot of the book doing field work and living unpleasantly along the backroads of Texas. But the circumstances of the story are secondary to the boy-man, son-father relationship. You don't find many Texas writers who can face the bitter reality of rural poverty in a changing society as Stilwell does, and this book is one of those rare, unduplicated Texas works that convinces the reader it speaks for thousands of others . . . call it cynicism, or whatever. Some who knew Stilwell better than I did—and I didn't know him well at all— say his streak of frustration and cynicism kept him from being the greater writer he should have been. I'm neutral, but *The Uncovered Wagon* is evidence enough that Texas benefitted when he did put his angry heart in it.

The Comanche Barrier to South Plains Settlement

by RUPERT NORVAL RICHARDSON

Arthur H. Clark, Glendale, California, 1933

This is straightforward history, done well and done professionally by a writer I consider the equal to any historian the Southwest has produced. *The Comanche Barrier* is not a history of the Comanche Indian tribes, but it does make enough investigations into the tribal past to satisfy questions about how this one group of Indians became the scourge and terror of Texans, even as their numbers (never great) were being crushed to a remnant. Richardson's scholarship works exactly the way a reader wants it to: it fills in the gaps, it informs you when the scene is clouded, and it supports its contentions and conclusions. *The Comanche Barrier* is a model of historical viewing and information. Dr. Richardson, who was born in 1891 in West Texas while the frontier was still very much alive around him, does not slide off into ancestral praise and aboriginal condemnation; his eye is constantly upon his topic, and that other "I," the first person pronoun, is not once used by the author. Only in the final paragraph of *The Comanche Barrier* does he let a few words of the romantic (which, in reality, any good historian should be) come through: "They were finally defeated in the unequal conflict, but what a magnificent fight they made! . . . But even yet, if we look by the light of an August moon across a Texas prairie dotted here and there by gnarled mesquite and mottes of scrubby oak, surely we shall see phantom warriors riding as of old—Comanches."

The Inheritors

by PHILIP ATLEE

Dial Press, New York, 1940

In 1940 there weren't many books being written about contemporary Texas, other than poor farmer or Depression novels; although, by then Texas had turned a corner very few of its residents (and virtually none of its writers) recognized: Texas had become an urban state. I did detailed research at the University of Texas (at Austin) in 1968 and found October 1928 as the exact month when Texas swung to having more people living in cities and towns than on farms, ranches, or other rural locations. In *The Inheritors* Philip Atlee (James Phillips) wrote about the urban scene in Fort Worth. This isn't "Cowtown." These are the young social sets—carousing, driving big cars too fast, going from party to country club to any kind of devilment and eventual crackups—physical and mental. It's an overindulged generation. One scathing chapter has this lost tribe out on the Fort Worth dump at night shooting rats for thrills, they're so bored with the usual run of fornication, drunkenness, and bragging about daddy's money. The story is well done—thirty or forty years before its time. Few Texas books have been able to repeat the harsh dismay, the inspired brutality of *The Inheritors*.

I'LL DIE BEFORE I'LL RUN

✪

The Story of
the Great Feuds of Texas

by
C. L. SONNICHSEN

HARPER & BROTHERS PUBLISHERS
New York

I'll Die Before I'll Run
The Story of the Great Feuds of Texas
by C. L. SONNICHSEN
Harper & Brothers, New York, 1951

Forget all that cheap fiction about Texas and Indian fights, the real hair-raisers were the feuds among the old Texans themselves. And the feuds covered the state, from Teneha and Timpson to El Paso and Laredo. (Laredo was the only place where a *cannon* was used in a Texas feud.) But Leland is a historian, not a fictioneer. *I'll Die Before I'll Run* is well documented and as close to the truth as a feud can be pinned down. In fact, even after the passage of a century or more, some of the feuds can't be safely discussed around the old feuding grounds: all the issues still haven't been decided. Sonnichsen once told me he was *persona non grata* in a few odd places (which he'd rather not name) because of his book. *I'll Die Before I'll Run* has been pilfered for stories by magazine and adventure book writers without due credit. I'll confess, I've even pilfered a tiny piece, but with proper thanks. Sonnichsen brought it on himself by being so reliable, yet so readable.

SIX YEARS WITH THE TEXAS RANGERS

1875 TO 1881

BY

JAMES B. GILLETT

Ex-Sergeant Company "A," Frontier Battalion

Von Boeckmann-Jones Co., Publishers
Austin, Texas

Six Years With the Texas Rangers
by JAMES B. GILLETT
Yale University Press, New Haven, 1925

I read *Six Years With the Texas Rangers* in high school for an unusual, but trivial, reason: I discovered James B. Gillett and I shared the same birth date, November 4. I attached a mystical significance to November 4, so I was excited to read something written by someone born on "my" birthday. (I am not an astrology believer of great depth, but being a Scorpio, I cannot escape an interest in the pseudo-science. Scorpios get hit too often to disregard their astral inheritance.) Of course, I sensed at once that our common birth date had nothing to do with the quality of Gillett's story. It is superb, and truthful; its dramatic color coming from the events themselves, not Gillett's manner of telling them. Even Walter Prescott Webb's *The Texas Rangers* (held to be the definitive work on same) doesn't pack as much of the aura of Ranger service. Gillett joined the Rangers in 1875 at age 18, but he never succumbs to the deification process so many other writers (including Webb) stumble through when recalling those gods of the frontier. Gillett is careful, but not academic. I ran across him again years later when writing a book about Herman Lehmann, the captive Texas boy who became, for all purposes, an Indian. Herman and Gillett fought one another and Herman, in a manner of speaking, won the fight—but the men (both were boys at the fight) didn't meet each other until nearly fifty years later. I suggest you read the two November 4's, Gillett and Greene—*The Last Captive*—to get the whole story.

POEMS BY R. G. VLIET

EVENTS
&
CELEBRATIONS

NEW YORK : THE VIKING

Events and Celebrations
by R. G. VLIET
The Viking Press, New York, 1966

Texas has produced a lot of poetry, but not a lot of good poetry. R. G. Vliet, who has not lived in Texas for many years but who still considers himself a Texan (at least, he did the last time I discussed it with him), created a Texas poem which is purely a classic when he wrote "Clem Maverick." It catches the excitement and the sorrow of Texas modern country and western music—full of phoniness, full of hype, but sometimes full of real tears and blind heartache. Clem is a celebrated composer and C&W entertainer at the top of the charts—and although this poem was written before the big worldwide surge of country music, it doesn't miss a lick or stand a day outdated. It's about mankind's fantasies, not mankind's fads. The rest of the poems in *Events and Celebrations* aren't so completely identified with Texas as "Clem Maverick," but they are completely worthy.

DILLON ANDERSON

I and Claudie

An Atlantic Monthly Press Book
Little, Brown and Company · Boston · 1951

I and Claudie

by DILLON ANDERSON

Little, Brown, Boston, 1951

When Clint Hightower (the "I") and his sidekick Claudie first appeared in *Atlantic Monthly*, I had been given a subscription as a graduation present a short time before and despaired of ever seeing Texas humor in such an august journal. It was enough, for me, that they were picaresque (haven't you always wanted to have a genuine occasion to use that word, after hearing it all the way from 9th-grade through graduate school?), but in addition, it was Texas they roamed, conning their way, a pair of up-to-date Gentle Grafters, outsmarting bankers and oilmen, but almost as often falling victim to their own softheartedness or their own cleverness. Years later, I discovered Dillon Anderson was not some ink-stained wretch but was a highly successful Houston corporate lawyer. I eventually met him at a Texas Institute of Letters dinner in Houston, but it was one of those, "Hello, I've always liked your work. . ." kind of meetings, and he died before I had the chance (or the nerve) to sit down with him and explain why I wished he had been a flop as a lawyer so he could have done nothing but write. (That's a real artistic problem —do you owe your family the duty of a certain kind of upkeep that takes you away from your typewriter, or do you owe posterity the deeper obligation of your time? Someone once said to Texas Governor Oran Roberts that the State owed it to posterity to create a university, and he replied, "Dad gum it, I *am* posterity!")

Great River
The Rio Grande in North American History
by PAUL HORGAN
Rinehart & Co., New York, 1954, 2 vols.

Some historians have picked on this book for being more fictional than historical. They haven't meant it was untrue so much as it was written like a novel—the birth of a river, the ages and stories of the civilizations that lived along it—everything flowing along like a river of plot as well as water. That is exactly what I like about it. It finds the romance of that essentially lonesomest river in North America, the Great River, Rio Bravo, Rio Grande del Norte . . . its names almost interchangeable. For my part, I prefer Horgan's history to his fiction, although there are passages within his individual books that can't be surpassed for mood and sensual feeling. Unfortunately, most of these passages occur in his novels about New Mexico, not Texas. But *Great River* is a Texas book, despite Horgan's preference for the Indian and Latin cultures of the river's upper course. Texans are offended when it is suggested that the Rio Grande is not completely accepted as an all-Texas stream. Once, high in the Colorado Rockies, I straddled the little rivulet that a sign stated was the Rio Grande. What I did when I straddled it was beneath the dignity of a grown man (and I *was* a grown man), but I couldn't help feeling that being a Texan, by God, I had a right to do whatever I wanted to do with the *Reeo-Grandy* wherever I found it.

Sironia, Texas

by MADISON COOPER

Houghton Mifflin, Boston, 1952

I was in the book business in Abilene when this massive 1,731-page, two-volume novel was published, and I pushed it into the libraries of several customers before I'd read a word of it because of two romantic reports: the Houghton salesman told me it was a Waco, Texas, version of *Gone With the Wind*, and a former Waco resident said she used to pass the Cooper mansion late at night (it was a great, towered Victorian thing) and see a light high up in one spire where Madison, the Cooper scion, was tapping (or scribbling) out this enormous story of the hidden lives of a town. (It's working title was *Ugh!*) At the time of publication it was said to be the longest American novel ever published. At any rate, when I finally read a set before I sold it, I found it compelling, a Texas fiction unlike anything done before; more mysterious and Southern than Western, and as much the story of two black servants (a boy and a girl taken through adulthood) as the white Lipscomb dynasty they served. Madison Cooper died before he had a chance to develop the body of literature he obviously contained. Incidentally, he died while on the Baylor University track jogging. Writers, beware.

A Woman of the People
by BENJAMIN CAPPS
Duell-Sloan-Pearce, New York, 1966

Ben Capps is another Texas writer I'm happy to say I got in on the ground-floor of (if it's all right to preposition a sentence that way). His first book I saw, *The Trail to Ogallala*, created rising expectations in me (I was a book reviewer) which were rapidly fulfilled. But none of his works can surpass *A Woman of the People*. The woman of the title is Helen Morrison, an Anglo girl, captured by the Comanches at a tender age and renamed (and reborn as) Tehanita—or, Little Texas Girl. The book is written in documentary style, although it is fiction, and Tehanita becomes so real that you are ready to look her up and compare her with Cynthia Ann Parker. But Capps has not done a blood-and-thunder (or blood-and-sex) Indian captive story. It is starkly psychological, Tehanita's struggle, after years of being an Indian warrior's wife and an Indian mother, to decide whether to return to her white family or stay with the dying prairie culture as it goes to an Oklahoma reservation. It is a work of high fictional art, not only in the adaptation of an Anglo writing talent to an Indian situation, but in the gaining of a woman's perception of her turmoil by a male author.

The Raven

by MARQUIS JAMES

Bobbs-Merrill, Indianapolis, 1929

My grandmother, who was the Carnegie librarian when I was growing up, told me not to read *The Raven* until I was "grown" because it would tell me things about Sam Houston, whose biography it is, that would disappoint me in him. So I didn't. But when I went to Enid, Oklahoma to attend Phillips University, I found Marquis James, who spent his boyhood there, to be the city's cultural hero, topping even Sherman Billingsley, the Enidite who ran (who *was*) that famous New York night spot, the Stork Club. So, having turned eighteen, I felt it my civic duty to read *The Raven*. And I was delighted. It is melodramatic, but only as melodramatic as any biography of "I Am" Houston must be—and the melodrama is backed up with a plethora of scholarly notes. It's Sam with the dirty rawhide on, but not a juiced-up revisionist's debunking. It's excellent history. My grandmother's warning probably came from the fact that Houston's liaison with Tiana Rogers, his Cherokee "wife," offended her moral code. Llerena Friend some years later wrote a carefully detailed biography, *Sam Houston, The Great Designer*, which gives primary emphasis to Houston's political and diplomatic schemes. It and *The Raven* make a nice pairing.

ADVENTURES
OF A
BALLAD HUNTER

By JOHN A. LOMAX

Sketches by Ken Chamberlain

THE MACMILLAN COMPANY

New York · 1947

Adventures of a Ballad Hunter
by JOHN A. LOMAX
Macmillan, New York, 1947

John Avery Lomax was raised in Bosque County, Texas, with a branch of the Chisholm Trail going past his front door. Many a morning, he later wrote, he was wakened by a cowboy singing to the herd. Unlike most Texans of that day, Lomax realized he was seeing, and hearing, the last citizens of a mythic world. By the time he started to college in 1887 at age twenty, he had devoted much of his time to the words and tunes from the grand era of the cowboy. The eventual result was *Cowboy Songs* in 1910—the foundation of western folk music. But in later years Lomax began collecting Negro folk blues and work songs of East Texas and the South, and with his youngest son, Alan, made a monumental series of recordings—by means of direct-cut discs and an overly burdened Ford car—going into the fields, the homes, and the prisons for black singers. His most famous discovery was Lead Belly (Hudie Ledbetter), whom Lomax petitioned to freedom from a life term for murder in Louisiana. All this is told without embellishment, but with immense readability in *Adventures of a Ballad Hunter*, which was published shortly before the death of a Texan who recognized the importance of one of the commonest occurrences of his boyhood.

Leaving Cheyenne
by LARRY MCMURTRY
Harper & Row, New York, 1963

This may draw some argument, but I think *Leaving Cheyenne* is Larry McMurtry's best writing—the first half of it, at least. His description of the old North Fort Worth cattle world, about the time of World War I, with the stockyards, the cowboy hotels, cattle trains pulling in every hour, the sound of streetcars, and bootheels on paving bricks, delivers such an absolute sense of time and place it is shocking to remember McMurtry was in his twenties (and fifty years had gone) when he wrote it. A complicated love story fills the last portion of *Leaving Cheyenne*, and brings the novel up to modern times. The writing is well delivered, but I've never been able to balance it against that superb beginning. (Moviemakers were not able to do as much with the love story, either, in *Loving Mollie*.) Frankly, I flipped a mental coin with myself choosing *Leaving Cheyenne* over McMurtry's *Moving On*. The fact that *Moving On* is a contemporary story of Texas urban life (mostly) has an especial appeal for me. But, as before, I believe *Leaving Cheyenne* is better written. (Why *Cheyenne* in an altogether Texas novel? The title comes from the cowboy song, "Goodbye, Old Paint." John Lomax says it was the last waltz at a cowboy ball: "The 'fiddle' is silenced and the entire company sing as they dance.")

Horse Tradin'

by Ben K. Green, d.v.m.

Alfred A. Knopf, New York, 1967

Angus Cameron, that noblest of all New York editors, called me in the summer of 1965 and asked if I were kin to a Dr. Ben Green. I said no, after briefly discounting the significance of the final *e* on my name when it comes to claiming kin. Angus said I was the loser, because Green had written a story ("Gray Mules") in *Southwest Review* that was a classic. He suggested I call Ben, which I did. This began a literary adventure I am not likely to repeat, because there can only be one Ben Green in a lifetime. Although I was closer to him than anyone in the book world, I never uncovered the real Ben Green. I never tried. But I had a unique triumph: he never got mad at me. Ben was a spellbinder—he admitted, with charming haste, he knew more about horses than any person alive (I believed it). He became, on publication of *Horse Tradin'*, a major writer—yet most of his fellow writers would not admit it. Why? Because he was also hardheaded, vain, perverse, dissembling, and impossibly cantankerous at times. For example, those D.V.M. initials on *Horse Tradin'* never appeared on another Green book because they were false. He tried to hide the fact that he had served time in Huntsville, that he had been married, and that he was relatively young—at least ten years younger than he looked. He was a glorious storyteller who got furious if you implied his stories were fiction—yet his writing in things like *The Shield Mares* proves his humanity was greater than he could face. He loved my wife and once sent a fellow 150 miles to plant a special peach tree he was giving her. When he died, I cried. I couldn't help it.

Goodbye to a River
by JOHN GRAVES
Alfred A. Knopf, New York, 1960

I was a newsman covering the annual meeting of the West Texas
Historical Association in 1958 when a non-historian speaker told of
taking a canoe trip down the Brazos River, flavoring his talk with
history, folklore, and bits of natural philosophy. Over lunch he
told me *Holiday* magazine was using a feature he'd written about
that trip, and a few months later I discovered *Atlantic Monthly* de-
voting its cover to his fiction piece, "The Last Running"—so by
the time the book, *Goodbye to a River*, came out in the fall of 1960, I
was already acquainted with John Graves and his work. But friend-
ship had nothing to do with my recognition that *Goodbye to a River*
is a great book (and I have my review, done on publication, to back
me up.) It contains the essential humor, the rawness, and earthy
wisdom of an old, rural Texas society without sacrificing intelli-
gence and historical accuracy. There have been only a handful of
books that achieved this plateau. *Goodbye to a River* alerts the reader,
from page one, to the fact that this is a masterly work, worthy of
almost any literary comparison. I rank it the finest piece of Texas
writing ever done, but, for once, won't insist everyone else agree.
Incidentally, if "The Last Running" were a bit longer than a story,
I would list it among the best books. It's worthy.

50 *The Uncovered Wagon* 50

Interwoven

Afterword

The Raven

50 *Texas History Movies* 50

A Personal Country
by A. C. GREENE
Alfred A. Knopf, New York, 1969

This odyssey of West Texas is a classic and a worthy companion to John Graves' *Goodbye to a River*. If the list of best Texas books were reduced to but ten, *A Personal Country* would still make the cut. It is that good, a notable landmark for any writer to leave, and it reads better today, thirteen years after it was first published, than it did when Greene finished the manuscript at Paisano. Like jerky and whiskey and tobacco, it cures well, and the older you get the more you appreciate it. It is the voice that holds you. It is a perceptive voice, as intelligent as the land it describes is broad, and it speaks with a flat, prairie honesty that is profoundly American, out of the old rock.

Listen to Greene speak:

"I knew, for the first time, how much the place and the past had created in my people what influenced me through them. I thought of the size and shape of the experiences that had made me and I wondered where and why it all began. How much of me was red dirt, was sand hills and long, empty plains? What was born of slow-spoken closemindedness, gained from a frontier brush-arbor camp meeting, or what was begun in a dugout where a young girl looked in fright and hatred at the wilderness around her?

"And I began to see something beyond the land and beyond my blood with the land in it. . . ."

And so he takes us with him "on a billowy ocean of land" where there was "isolation in the grass and in the wind."

In *A Personal Country*, Greene works the same theme as Graves did in *River*. It is the conflict between inertia and movement.

The movement seems a contradiction at first. To those of us who don't know it well, West Texas seems to be a bedrock of constancy, physically and metaphysically, even in a human sense. The fossils are not limited to geology. And yet fossils themselves are evidence of the cycle of life and death and rejuvenation. Nothing really remains put on Graves' river or in Greene's country, not even the dreams that would keep things as they used to be. The river changes and is changed. The winds blow, the grass surges and dies, the windmills whine and topple. Babies are born and old folks die, towns crop up and decay away, the young people leave and the codgers hang on. It is all here, time, place, treasure, blood, sex, success, failure, death and, of course, god and the devil and grief, and the going on, as people must.

The Alfred A. Knopf editions are out of print, but Texas A & M Press has seen fit to re-issue *A Personal Country*, complete with Ancel Nunn's memorable illustrations which accompanied the original.

Bill Porterfield

Designed by David Holman at the Wind River Press
The text type is Van Dijck monotype with Arrighi titling
Offset edition on Booktext paper
by BookCrafters, Inc., Michigan